Learning From Bees

A Philosophy of Natural Beekeeping

by
Philip Chandler
author of
The Barefoot Beekeeper

Copyright © 2012 Philip Chandler
All Rights Reserved

Off The Bookshelf Edition
December 2012

Foreword

Although I have been a lover of the natural world for as long as I can remember, it was not until the late 1990's that I became particularly interested in bees.

At that time, I was active in the campaign against the open-field growing of genetically manipulated plants and it became increasingly clear to me that emergent bio-technologies and their associated herbicides and insecticides would one day pose a serious threat to organic agriculture, to wild plants and therefore to pollinating insects. It was also apparent that the agri-bio-pharma corporations promoting GM had no interest in the conservation of natural eco-systems and would most likely use their growing economic power to overturn environmental protection laws, forcing governments to accept their demands by fair means or foul. Sadly, those fears have been shown to have been well-founded.

When I took up beekeeping, I discovered that the same people who were selling insecticides to farmers were also selling similar chemicals to beekeepers. Rather than being a gateway into the natural world, beekeeping had become largely a matter of maintaining stocks by means of synthetic medications. Further enquiries led me to conclude that 'modern' beekeeping methods and toxic agricultural practices were largely to blame for the massive increase in bee diseases and parasite problems reported during the 20th century,

I decided to find a better way to interact with bees, which led me to study older and simpler methods of bee husbandry. After experimenting with various types, shapes and sizes of beehive, I settled on a simple top bar hive design that was easy to build and required no manufactured parts or precise dimensions. With a few minor modifications, this is the hive I still favour.

In 2007 I wrote *The Barefoot Beekeeper*, which set

out my challenge to the world of conventional beekeeping and offered an alternative paradigm. It soon became apparent that other people had been thinking along similar lines, and when bees were headlined month after month in the national press, following the outbreak of so-called 'colony collapse disorder' in the USA, many more people became interested in bees and what became known as the 'natural beekeeping' movement began to emerge.

This term is, admittedly, paradoxical: keeping bees is not 'natural', but it is the negotiation of this paradox that generates conversation and gives the movement its energy and diversity. We tend to avoid books of rules and prefer to be guided by principles. We encourage observation and interaction with the natural world. We remind beekeepers that there are many other pollinator species in need of protection. Natural beekeeping is a process, not a destination.

Along the way, we are discovering much about ourselves and our connections with each other, with the Earth and with nature, and learning to value bees for what they are and what they do, rather than what they produce.

Since those early days, I have spent a good deal of my time observing, thinking and experimenting, looking for more nature-friendly and less invasive ways to observe, work with and support the remarkable honeybee. Some of these experiments have produced useful innovations and ideas and all were successful in the sense that I learned something from each of them - very often about what *not* to do.

You will find practical, 'how-to' instructions in my other books: this is a collection of my thoughts about bees and beekeeping, in the hope that you find some of them interesting and stimulating.

Phil Chandler
December 2012

Contents

5	Bees and Flowers: a Perfect Partnership
11	The Nature of Bees
23	What is Natural Beekeeping?
31	Balanced Beekeeping
38	The Importance of Drones
42	Do You Really Want to Keep Bees?
47	The Beatrix Potter Syndrome
55	The Bigger Picture
60	Sustaining The Honeybee
66	Asking Questions
69	Advice to Inventive Beekeepers
71	Inner Beekeeping
76	Learning From Bees
80	Ten Things You Can Do

Bees and Flowers: a Perfect Partnership

If you have spent much time among flowering plants, you will have noticed the comings and goings of numerous insects. Some of them seem to pay little attention to the flowers themselves, while others are clearly attracted to them and spend much of their time flying from one to another, intent on their own, private business.

Among these myriad insects, the most noticeable - for their size, their sound and their industry - are the bees; especially the bumblebees and honeybees. Bumblebees are the bigger, louder and hairier types, which forage earlier and later in the day and in the year, while honeybees are slimmer, more streamlined and in some places, more numerous, as soon as the spring flowers show themselves and the daytime temperature reaches 9 or 10 degrees centigrade.

Co-evolution

Bees and flowering plants have evolved together, perhaps for as long as 130 million years. Bees and numerous other insects are the primary pollinators of many of our native and un-hybridized garden plants. Bees are totally dependent on flowers for food, while the plants rely on insects to be present at the right time to pass pollen from anthers to stamens to ensure fertilization and thus the continuation of their species. Without flowers, the bees would starve; without bees, the flowers would fail to set seed. About 90% of all flowering plants require the help of insects with their reproductive process. Some involve birds, bats and butterflies, but bees are by far the most important pollinators of our fruit and vegetable crops.

Most of the wild flowers we see around us in meadows and hedgerows are there only because they have formed successful relationships with bees. They have learned to produce nectar to attract the attention of bees, which provide a pollination service as a by-product of their feeding habits.

Many flowers have patters of colour that act as 'runway lights' for bees, which see better towards the ultra-violet end of the spectrum than we do. Poppies, for example, have patterns on their petals that can only be seen by us under ultra-violet light.

Pollination

In October 2010, the United Nations published a report, in which they place a value on insect pollination at £134 billion (153bn Euros). A significant portion of this pollination service is provided by bees.

Honeybees have a long and intimate association with many of our fruit crops. Apples are an obvious example, as beehives are often placed in orchards. Wild bees do some of the work, but yields in commercial orchards are greatly increased by the addition of honeybees, because they live in such large communities and are present early in the year in the numbers that are needed for large-scale pollination. According to tests made back in the 1920s, the difference in yields between orchards where honeybees are placed and those without added honeybees can be at least four times and as much as eighteen times. If you are a gardener, a smallholder or homesteader, the chances are that whatever flowering crops you are growing are already being pollinated quite effectively by wild bees and other insects and unless you grow top fruit on a large scale, adding honeybees to the mix will have only a marginal effect on yields. Exceptions to this might include areas where neighbours routinely spray their crops with insecticides and places where wild bee populations have suffered for other reasons, such as heavy pollution. Unfortunately, in either of these cases, you are probably in the wrong place to keep honeybees.

Fertilization occurs within the flower when the

male gamete unites with the female egg in the ovary. Once it is complete, the fruit develops. Most top fruit requires pollination to ensure that fruit 'sets' properly, which can be judged, in the case of apples, by the number of seeds present in maturing fruit. There should be between seven and ten seeds if pollination has been fully effective. If there were not enough pollinators present when the flowers were in bloom, the result is misshapen fruit that often falls before it is ripe.

The almond industry in California, which produces 80% of the world's almonds, is completely dependent on honeybees for pollination, as they are the only pollinators available in sufficient quantity to service the vast number of almond trees present in that area. This requires the transportation of around a million hives - half of all the honeybees in the USA - often thousands of miles across country for several days at a stretch. Servicing this massive mono-crop causes immense stress to honeybee colonies.

Pollen in the hive

Honeybees gather pollen and take it back to their hives by collecting it in their 'pollen baskets'; specially-adapted hairs on their rear pair of legs. In the hive, it is mixed with nectar to form what we call 'bee-bread'. After a short period of fermentation, this becomes food for the nurse bees looking after young larvae and for the queen's attendants. They need the extra nutrition it provides to enable them to make 'royal jelly', a secretion of the hypopharyngeal glands located in the heads of worker bees.

During the process of foraging, some pollen grains stick to hairs on the bee's body, and are transferred to the stamens of another flower. This is the mechanism by which most pollination occurs.

Pollen contains protein, vitamins, minerals, sugars, fats, fatty acids, enzymes, hormones and other substances, the proportions of which vary according to the host species.

While it may be a valuable food supplement for humans, it is of central importance to bee nutrition.Like us, bees do best on a varied diet, and the best thing you can do for them as a gardener is to encourage a wide range of wild and native flowers.

Bumblebees also gather pollen, although not in the same quantity as honeybees, because they live in much smaller colonies; rarely more than a hundred individuals. A honeybee colony in mid summer may contain 50,000 workers plus five or six thousand drones.

Apart from being present in large numbers early in the year, another significant reason that honeybees are so important as pollinators is the sheer variety of flowers they are willing to visit: over 600 different species. Of the other bees, only *Bombus terrestris* comes close, with about 360 favoured species, while three others - *agrorum*, *hortorum* and *lapidarius* - visit around 250 each.

While wasps, butterflies, moths, hoverflies and many others do contribute their efforts to pollination, bees are so important to flowers because they feed exclusively, throughout their lives, on flower products. Wasps take nectar during the spring, but obtain most of their protein from sources, such as the larvae of other insects, including bees. Flies and butterflies live rather short lives and therefore their contribution to pollination is fleeting.

Planting for bees

Honeybees and bumblebees have a considerable overlap in the range of flowers they visit, but some are largely ignored by honeybees - notably honeysuckle and red clover - because their probosces are too short to reach the nectar. If you are mainly interested in providing habitat for bumblebees, you will be able to find lists of their favourite flowers, or you can observe them to see which flowers they prefer.

You don't need to think in terms of planting exclusively for bees, as they will range far and wide over a large area, but if you bear in mind that they will have a preference for plants that yield nectar as well as pollen and that they need food from early spring right through to the onset of winter, you can let this guide your choice of plants for your garden. Aim for variety, and choose plants that are close to their wild, natural state, as many double-flowered hybrids produce nothing for bees. Aim for a long flowering season, with both early and late blossoms. Bees start looking for food as soon as it is warm enough for them to fly and will forage on the odd warm days in winter.

No chemicals

To ensure your garden is truly bee-friendly, one of the most important things you can do is avoid using toxic sprays against so-called pests. In particular, avoid using any systemic insecticides, especially those containing neonicotinoids, which have been shown to be extremely toxic to bees even in minute doses. Be vigilant when you buy packaged garden compost, as some products may contain Imidacloprid as a vine weevil treatment. Such compost may kill earthworms as well as any insects that come into contact with it.

By nurturing your soil health; encouraging bees, hoverflies and other insects and avoiding the use of synthetic chemicals, you will allow your garden to reach a natural balance between predators and prey that will keep 'pest' species under natural control. You may want to talk to any of your neighbours who habitually use sprays or toxic lawn dressings and persuade them that a healthy insect population is far more important than having a perfect, weed-free garden.

The primary requisite for having bees in your garden is a chemical-free environment, rich in nectar- and pollen-producing plants. You will never be able to grow enough flowers in an average garden to feed a colony of honeybees, but by cultivating older varieties and leaving some areas unkempt, you will make a valuable contribution to their habitat and to the welfare of the wild bees and many other creatures in your area.

The Nature of Bees

Before we can consider any form of 'bee keeping', we must make some attempt to understand the nature of the creature we will be dealing with.

The conventional approach to this subject invariably begins with pictures of individual bees: you will find many books with diagrams and photographs of dissected honeybees, showing how their anatomy is arranged and how parts of a dead bee appear under a microscope. I recommend you take a look through at least one of them so you have an idea how all the bits fit together and what they all do.

However, as natural beekeepers - and as observers of and participants in living nature - we are not so much interested in dead bees as in living ones. And as soon as we decide to look at living honeybees, we have to think, not of individual bees, but in terms of the unit of survival: the colony.

In a very real and literal sense, honeybees can only exist as part of the large, extended family that is their colony. This is often referred to as a 'super-organism'.

This family consists of a mother, which we call the queen (although she is not a monarch or ruler in any sense), perhaps a dozen groups of half-sisters, who share a common mother but had different fathers (all deceased), and a band of brothers, who carry only their mother's genes as they had no fathers.

A rather confusing and somewhat unexpected picture, then, and one that we will begin to understand only by careful study of their unusual life cycle and unique behaviour.

Survival Instinct

The primary motivation of all creatures is, of

course, survival. This applies to all forms of life, down to the tiniest of of bacteria. The forms of life we see on Earth today are those that have succeeded in surviving by adapting to the constantly-changing climatic conditions our planet has experienced since its formation.

The fact that the ancestry of the honeybee can be traced back in the fossil records to at least 100 million years ago demonstrates that she is certainly a survivor and, therefore, an excellent adaptor to changing conditions.

Apis mellifera - the European honeybee - probably originated in Africa and spread throughout Europe and across Asia as far as the Siberian tundra, developing subspecies and local ecotypes to take advantage of the wide range of climates and flora she encountered.

Recently, fossil evidence has been found that proves she once had relatives in North America, which the species was formerly supposed not to have colonized. One day, the mystery of why she failed to thrive there may be solved.

Natural History

The evolutionary history of the honeybee is intimately entwined with that of the flowering plants: you could say they were made for each other.

Flowers provide food for bees and are rewarded with pollination services. Many other insects are involved in pollination, of course, but none has the honeybee's capacity to come through winter and build up so quickly and in such large numbers and be available to early-flowering plants and trees. It is this capability that makes the honeybee so commercially valuable as a pollinator of our fruit crops, as well as being essential to the survival of many wild flowering species.

Exactly how the honeybee evolved as a social creature and developed its remarkable ability to live co-operatively in huge groups remains a mystery. The observable fact is that they do so live, and this is what we are interested in: the actual behaviour of the honeybee colony as a collective, co-operative, highly successful, multi-component yet amazingly co-ordinated 'creature' that is entirely independent of man but now largely under our influence, playing a vital role in the production of some of our most valued foods, and exerting a remarkable degree of selection over many of the flowers that bloom in our gardens and natural landscapes.

The Swarm

So let's look at the honeybee colony at first as a swarm - a whirling, roaring cloud of bees, emerging from a hive or a hollow tree - a sight seen by few people nowadays, living out of touch with the natural world in cities and suburbia, but remembered by all who have witnessed it.

Despite its wild and anarchic appearance, which can cause panic in those unfamiliar with bee behaviour, a flying swarm is in fact purposeful and organized and not in the least interested in causing a nuisance to humans or anything else: their one aim is to find a suitable place in which to set up home.

This is the 'naked swarm' - a division of the colony, analogous to the division of a cell - which has left behind them in their old nest the beginnings of a new bee family. They now need a new protective 'shell' around them - which may be a hollow tree, a cosy loft space or a conveniently placed beehive - some kind of cavity that will protect them from the weather and from predators.

The swarm is the macro-reproductive mechanism of the honeybee, by which they generate new colonies and claim new territory; as compared with the mating of the queen and her laying of individual eggs, which is the micro-reproductive system, operating within individual colonies.

When a colony reaches a certain size and is likely to out-grow its home - and the bees believe that there will be sufficient forage for them to establish a new colony and provide it with winter stores - the queen will be guided by her retinue to lay fertilized eggs into special cells that have been prepared purely for the purpose of raising new queens. Unlike the horizontal - or rather, slightly upwardly-inclined - cells in which her eggs are normally deposited, she must now lay into a larger, vertically-hanging wax cell, generously provided with the substance we call 'royal jelly'. This highly nutritious and complex food contains - among many other compounds - a protein called 'royalactin', which recent research [Nature (2011) doi:10.1038/nature10093] reveals to be at least partly responsible for altering the activity within the egg so as to produce a fertile queen rather than an infertile worker bee.

During the swarming season - early to mid-summer in temperate climates - six or more of these cells may be prepared and each provided with an egg. After three days, a larva will hatch from the egg and feed eagerly and - because she is to be a mother - exclusively on royal jelly, topped up from glands in the heads of young workers who have themselves fed on 'bee bread', comprising pollen fermented in nectar. Worker and drone larvae are only allowed to eat royal jelly for three days, after which they are put on less concentrated rations for a further five days until they are sealed in their wax tombs, to be reborn after a 12-day metamorphosis.

The queen larva gains weight rapidly on her special diet and after five more days in the open, her cell is sealed by her attendants and she is left for a further seven days to undergo the metamorphosis from larva to pupa to emerging imago.

A few days before the first queen cell is capped, the bees become restless and - if conditions are judged to be right - a collective decision is made to send out a swarm.

The current laying queen, having had her food rations reduced to enable her to lose enough weight to fly, is hustled towards the entrance. Together with up to two thirds of the colony's mature bees, which have filled their stomachs with honey in preparation for comb-building, she flies out and joins the excited, circling throng. In deference to her still limited flight capacity, they may travel only a few yards from their home before settling on the limb of a nearby tree, where the great cluster gathers around the queen to form a temporary, protective shell.

At this stage, their queen is especially precious: if she should perish, swarming will have been in vain and they would have no choice but to return to their old hive. Here on the branch they will stay for a few hours or, if necessary, a few days, while scouts are sent out to look for a suitable new home. If it rains, or turns cold, they will cluster tightly together, heads pointing upwards and wings arranged like the scales on a reptile, so as to shed water and retain heat. While they are so clustered, it is possible gently to stroke a hand over the backs and wings of the bees, almost as if they were the fur on a cat. This is the one time when it is easy to perceive the colony as a single, mammal-like macro-organism.

Scout bees search the surrounding terrain for potential homes. They will fly around, enter and measure the volume of promising cavities, assessing them for suitability in ways only bees understand. They report back to the suspended colony if they become excited by a particular location, conveying their degree of enthusiasm by means of a version of the 'waggle dance', performed on the surface of the swarm, sending vibrations throughout the cluster.

A number of scouts return with news of their finds and a collective decision is reached - by some means that puts national governments and executive committees to shame - as to which scout has been successful in finding their ideal home. Once a decision has been made, the colony rises in a purposeful cloud and makes directly for their chosen residence, moving in without further delay.

Comb Building

At this point, the bees are in an excited, feverish

state, and from this they produce heat. This is the second requirement for extruding wax from glands on the underside of their abdomens in order to commence construction of their 'skeleton' - the beeswax comb - that will be both a nursery and a food store for the next several years, if they remain undisturbed. A swarm that has clustered on a branch for a day or two will often leave the beginnings of wax comb behind, such is their eagerness to begin building.

Hanging from the roof of the cavity, they join legs to form chains, measuring up to construct their honeycomb according to their own particular geometry. Tiny flakes of soft, malleable wax are kneaded together into precise, hexagonal tubes, offset at their bases and slightly inclined upwards towards their open ends, to enclose the greatest possible volume of space for the minimum amount of precious wax. The slight slope is calculated, it seems, so as to hold by surface tension the greatest volume of nectar that can be contained in a cell that must, at other times, serve as a womb for developing larvae. It is this extraordinarily economical use of a material that is so costly in energy terms to manufacture, that has enabled the honeybee to thrive in such a variety of conditions and cavities for so long.

Once a single comb is well under way, another parallel comb is started close by on each side, at the precisely-calculated distance to allow cell-packers and nurse bees to work comfortably back-to-back.

The first priority is to build up a strong population of worker bees, which will become the foraging force so vital to the growth and survival of the new colony. As soon as space is available, the queen is guided by her escorts to lay a fertilized egg in each of the empty cells nearest to the centre of the new comb, working in a spiral pattern. The middle of each comb will soon be full of brood in all stages, and three weeks after the first egg is laid, new workers will begin to emerge from their cells and take over the nursing duties of their now elderly sisters, who may return to foraging duty for their few remaining days of life. Foraging is exhausting work and worker bees live for only a few weeks: those who flew with the swarm must ensure that the next generation is well established before they expire.

Queen Mating

Meanwhile, back in the old colony from which our swarm flew, the first of the new queens has emerged, a week after her cell was sealed. A decision has been made by the colony that she will take over from her mother, and consequently she has stung to death all her potential rival queens, still in their cells. Their bodies will be dragged out of the hive and disposed of by workers and her sting will never be used again.

In five or six days, in the warmth of a summer's afternoon, the virgin queen flies from her family accompanied by a handful of worker escorts and travels to a place known only to bees, perhaps two or three kilometres away, where she will mate with a dozen drones from among the hundreds gathered there from other colonies. They have all navigated to that spot by reading clues in the landscape that they cannot have learned from their fathers (for they have no fathers) or their sisters (workers have no time to spare for such things). Tiny particles of magnetite in their bodies aid their navigation and their congregation areas may be located over anomalies in the Earth's magnetic field.

Dodging swifts and swallows, with the help of her escorts acting as decoys, the queen returns to her colony, soon to begin laying her eggs: fertilized eggs in the smaller cells, where her daughters will grow to form the workforce of the colony; unfertilized eggs in the larger cells, where they will become fertile males, with the potential to carry her genetic code to other virgin queens from distant colonies. Her sons are indeed her own, as they have no father, while her daughters, having many fathers between them, may show clear signs of their various paternal influences in their colouration.

She may take several mating flights until her spermatheca are full, and then she will not fly again until - perhaps the summer after next - she flies with a swarm of her own.

Supersedure

At the peak of her laying capacity, for a few weeks in summer, she may lay as many as three thousand eggs every day and may continue to be mother to the colony for a further three or four years. Sooner or later, though, she will become incapable of maintaining the needed rate of lay and the colony will make the decision to replace her by swarming, as they did her mother, or - usually towards the end of the season - by supersedure.

Unlike swarming, which may require many queen cells to be constructed in order to maximize the potential of macro-reproduction, supersedure may only require a single cell, most often large and centrally placed in a specially-constructed recess or hole in a comb. This will be the best queen a colony is capable of making, and much care goes into ensuring that she is first class, as the colony is investing everything in her: she must carry them through the winter or they will all perish.

Preparing for Dearth

The swarmed colony, now established in a new home, is building up well. The old queen has resumed laying, and the season moves on. The summer solstice passes and the bees note the shortening days. All their energy now goes into building up their stores to carry them through the winter: even though the summer foragers will never live to feel the cold weather, nor will they eat any of the stored honey, they know they have to work themselves to death for the sake of the survival of the colony.

Nectar and pollen are gathered from selected sources and passed from forager to house bee to be stored, carefully arranged, in cells best placed for their later use. At night, a gentle hum is heard coming from the colony, as ten thousand wings pass a current of warm air across the surface of the nectar-filled cells, evaporating excess water until it comprises less than one fifth of the volume of liquid, when it can be sealed up as honey without danger of fermentation.

Here we see clear evidence of the true nature of bees: they never behave as individuals with their own agendas, but always they labour selflessly for the greater good of their extended family. We see it again if they are disturbed by a predator - they will hurl themselves at their common foe, disembowelling themselves by leaving their stings behind in its flesh - with no thought for their individual selves, but only for the well-being of their colony.

Eviction of the Drones

Towards the end of summer, as the queen's rate of egg-laying slows to allow the population to adjust to its winter level, a collective decision is made that the drones - having had free passage since spring - are no longer required in the colony and are henceforth barred from entering. Those within the hive are hustled out by force, and any that resist are mercilessly put to death by stinging. Drones are only rarely carried through the winter - they appear to have no essential function at this time of year and would only eat valuable food that is needed by the workers. If the bees decide on a late-season supersedure, they will delay the eviction of the drones until the new queen is successfully mated, in case there are none available from other colonies. In fact, because drones travel freely from colony to colony, many of those present are likely to be from other families: this is one way the bees ensure genetic diversity, an essential characteristic of any successful species.

As the air temperature drops, the bees organize their food stores. They arrange to have plenty within easy reach above and to the sides of them and that there are no gaps that may become difficult to cross by the close-knit winter cluster, perhaps one fifth of its midsummer size. As the days shorten, foraging has stopped and the bees' metabolism has slowed. The cluster tightens and feeding is reduced to a minimum. Throughout the coldest part of winter, the queen stops laying, as there are enough bees to maintain some heat within the cluster and brood rearing would be a drain on precious resources.

All is quiet, until once more the days begin to lengthen and the air begins to warm, and the scent of the first spring flowers drifts into the hive.

In tropical zones, where there is no summer or winter, there are other conditions that dictate bees' food-gathering and reproductive behaviour, almost always including a part of the year when bees cannot forage. In hot, dry climates, there is a period of drought, when trees shed their leaves in order to save moisture, and other plants delay flowering until the rains arrive. In wet tropical areas, the monsoon season will keep bees indoors for the duration.

Colony Life

So our colony undergoes expansion, division and contraction, according to the availability of food, which is closely linked to the seasons and the local climate. Its only concern is its own survival, and to that end, individual bees will sacrifice themselves without a moment's hesitation, should they be called on to do so.

The colony has - as it were - 'phantom limbs' that reach out into the surrounding fields and hedgerows to seek food in quantities that are individually tiny but collectively substantial. They bring it back inside their collective 'body', where it is processed, amassed and sealed.

When its body outgrows its 'shell', it divides in two and the 'naked' part seeks another shell.

Such is the robust nature of its internal generative system that, should any harm come to a queen, a new one can quickly be made from any convenient, fertilized egg, by extending its cell and feeding it copious amounts of royal jelly. Such an 'emergency queen' will tide the colony over until it can make a perfect supersedure queen to ensure its continuance.

The colony survives all individuals and in that sense is potentially immortal. The huge variability contained in the genes of honeybees across their entire range is their insurance against disaster: within that gene pool is the potential to find a niche in which they can survive despite almost anything - save for mass poisoning - that may happen in the wider world.

Each colony - each 'collective creature' - develops its own variations of possible responses to intrusion. Anyone who has handled a number of hives will know that they all have particular 'personalities', from the most passive and co-operative to the most defensive and belligerent. Some will hardly respond at all to the gentle touch, while others may scamper all over the combs or fly into a violent rage at the slightest provocation. Some will keep themselves to themselves, while others will rob all nearby competitors of their stores and leave their victims to starve.

The bee keeper's work

Honeybees remain essentially unchanged by man, despite many attempts to selectively breed them. Their unique mating behaviour and reproductive cycle ensure that diversity and adaptability will continue to be the dominant themes in their evolution.

As I see it, our main job as bee keepers, or bee guardians, or bee herders, is to to be observant and to understand our bees to the best of our ability. We cannot fully enter into their world, but we have the opportunity to gain a greater appreciation of it. And once we fully understand how intimately embedded they are within the natural world and what sensitive indicators they are of disturbances to it, we may find ourselves unable to see the world again in a purely mechanistic way.

Having a deep appreciation of the interconnectedness of all living things leads us inevitably to the conclusion that we have a responsibility not only to the the bees but to everything that walks on the earth and flies in the air and shares this precious planet with us.

What is 'Natural Beekeeping?

The question should rather be, 'is any beekeeping natural?' As humans, our interest in them has been selfish: we have seen them as the source of a uniquely delicious, sweet substance and paid little heed to their pervasive presence in the natural world, where, largely unnoticed, they go about their business of farming flowers.

Farming?

It seems to me that bees are farmers. They have been carefully and skilfully selecting plants from among the available random mutations and crosses for more than 100 million years, while we have been dabbling in farming for a mere 10,000 or so. In the same way that growers select plant varieties for breeding, so have the bees and other pollinators selected, over tens of millions of years, the plants that provide them with food in the forms of pollen and nectar. By this means, they have greatly influenced the colours and patterns of our landscapes and the scents and flavours of the herbs and the hedgerow fruits that we have taken and developed into the food we eat.

Whether they conducted their selection work 'consciously', or it simply happened as a side-effect of their food-gathering activities, is a question to which we may never have a satisfactory answer; such is the case with many of the most innocent-sounding questions about bees. The best we can say is that, by focusing their attention on the flowers that produced the most nectar, or the nectar with optimum concentration of sugars, vitamins and minerals, or those which had the longest flowering season, or were most resilient to adverse weather - or whatever criteria they considered important that we cannot currently divine - they caused those plants to set more seed and so to flourish and spread, which is just what any farmer would do.

Honeybee evolution

In terms of practical understanding of nature, compared to the bees we are but infants. Before we turned up, they had flowers pretty much to themselves - give or take the odd herbivorous dinosaur - and they made a magnificent job of helping to create a recklessly varied biodiversity; never allowing one species to dominate and always ensuring that there would be, in the lands where they found it comfortable to live, something in flower that would provide them with sustenance at all possible times.

In cooler regions, honeybees learned to live in enclosed spaces, where they could control the temperature and humidity and protect their young from airborne diseases, with the help of resinous substances made by trees. They learned that, by visiting certain plants, they could gather sufficient quantities of nectar in the warm season to enable them to store it in concentrated form in sealed containers, where it would not spoil and so provide them with food to last them until the air again became warm and new flowers emerged.

They somehow understood that nectar was a watery substance and that containers for it had therefore to be impermeable to water, so they learned to make beeswax - the most water-proof substance in all the natural world - from glands in their own bodies. They understood the energy cost of manufacturing wax and so devised a system of cell construction that made the most efficient possible use of it; so it became, all at once, a larder and a nursery and a thermal reservoir and a sounding-board for their subtle, vibration-based communication system.

They became familiar with the effects of evaporation and condensation of water within the hive, learning to turn their living space into an efficient condenser in order to improve the recycling of water and the heat contained in it; at the same time reducing nectar to a more concentrated form of sugar, suitable for long-term storage.

Honeybees learned to defend themselves against predators by acting together, in the same way that they worked together to bring in food and nurse their young. They learned that the key to thriving in their world was to work along lines of least resistance, through co-operation and co-ordination with the seasonal changes. They had no need to claim territory for themselves at the expense of other species and so they had no need to waste energy on aggression: there was plenty for all.

Their cousins, the bumblebees, were able to fly in lower temperatures, due to their bulkier bodies and thicker fur, and were able to use their longer proboscuses to reach nectar in certain flowers that honeybees left alone. Other species adapted to a particular range of flowers that were in season just when they chose to become active, while some became partially carnivorous. And so, within the *Hymenoptera* order, the bees, ants and wasps diverged and adapted, each to their own ecological niche.

Honeybees focused on the advantages of living as a colony and their unique ability to reach out far into the surrounding landscape, concentrating and processing its sweetest and most delicate products within the space of their carefully laid-out nest. This made them more attractive to sweet-toothed predators, so they selected homes in hollow trees, well away from the ground, keeping their entrance small and well-protected by guards.

When humans appeared, they were for the most part just another minor nuisance, although they soon came armed with smoke and fire to claim their prize. Long before their arrival, bees had learned that the smell of smoke was a harbinger of fiery doom and that filling themselves with honey and evacuating their home was their only means of defence. Humans mistook this pre-evacuation behaviour for passivity and so began the habit of smoking bees before robbing them.

For tens of thousands of years, human interference in the lives of bees was limited to stealing honey from them once or twice per year. Most colonies escaped such attention, as they were inaccessible to these naked apes, who did not seem to be as clever at climbing trees as their hairy ancestors. Early attempts at keeping bees within reach, in order to rob them more easily, involved placing containers akin to sections of hollow tree, closer to the ground and making them attractive to passing swarms. Variations on this theme were employed by many cultures, according to locally-available materials: straw skeps were used in places where grain farming had been developed; reed baskets in the marshes; clay pots and pipes where sun was plentiful and rainfall low; logs and cork bark where such things grew freely and volcanic rock was hollowed out in the more geologically unstable areas. In all cases, the bees were mostly left to manage their own affairs until such time as some of their stores could profitably be robbed.

Bee farming

It was not until the advent of the movable-frame hive in the middle of the 19th century and the subsequent invention of the motor vehicle that bees' real problems with humans began. Revd. Langstroth's eponymous movable-frame hive, which - in tune with the Victorian *zeitgeist* - he regarded as fulfilling 'God's purpose' in giving man further mastery over nature, became the model upon which was based virtually every subsequent beehive design created with the intention of providing the beekeeper with a maximum yield of honey. His was the first really successful attempt at keeping honey separate from brood, such that honey could be harvested in bulk without fear of 'corruption' by eggs and developing larvae. It thus signalled the dawn of a new relationship between man and bees: that of master and servant.

Commercial beekeeping was born and came of age towards the end of the century with the introduction of self-powered trucks. Now it was easy to transport hives quickly and in large numbers to where crops were in flower, enabling the bee farmers (as they became known) to offer a mobile pollination service as well as to benefit from the harvests of honey.

Through the twentieth century, the scale of operations became substantially larger. In the USA, bee farmers controlling thousands - even tens of thousands - of hives became commonplace and the methods of the commercial honey producer were taught to and aped by the home beekeeper, who had no reason to question the knowledge of 'experienced' men. So we see to this day beginners being taught to check their hives every week for queen cells and to cut them out to prevent swarming; to mark queens with paint and clip their wings and to perform a number of other 'management' operations to exercise their 'God-given right' to control the lives of these wild insects.

Disease control

Meanwhile, a German conglomerate by the name of I. G. Farben - later Bayer - branched out from its core industry of fabric dyes into agricultural chemicals, derived from its development of chemical warfare products during World War I. They and others were soon making huge profits from the sale of insecticides and fertilizers.' Quick-fix' industrial agriculture was born and industrial-scale beekeeping followed swiftly in its wake.

However, along with the increase in scale came a commensurate increase in disease. From being a minor nuisance in the nineteenth century, foul brood became a serious threat, destroying huge numbers of colonies and resisting eradication. In Britain, during During WWII, Winston Churchill - himself a beekeeper - put in place the first Foul Brood Inspectors, in an effort to get the epidemic under control by the brutally simple strategy of destroying affected colonies, on the sound principle that removing susceptibility to disease from breeding stock will strengthen the survivors. The success of this approach is evidenced by the relative rarity of AFB outbreaks in Britain some 70 years later.

The other dread disease - the unrelated and somewhat less virulent European Foul Brood (EFB) - proved less easy to tackle and has become somewhat more common in recent years, largely due to earlier attempts to treat it with antibiotics.

Other diseases, such as *Nosema apis* and most recently *Nosema cerana* are endemic and the now almost ubiquitous parasitic mite *Varroa destructor*, with its assortment of vectored viruses, have taken a huge toll on the honeybee population in the last half century, despite a barrage of 'medications' that have' in all likelihood, made the problem worse.

Chemical failure

The tendency of the conventional beekeeping fraternity has been to throw yet more chemicals at a problem, in the hope that a 'magic bullet' will one day be found. To my mind, this is exactly the opposite of what needs to be done, since - as Einstein himself indicated - we will never solve such problems using the type of thinking that created them.

If, when Varroa was first discovered in Britain in 1992, we had done nothing but stop all imports of bees, ban all medications and allowed the bees to find their own way of dealing with the challenge, we would have lost a large number of colonies - perhaps nine out of ten - but by now, 20 years later, we would have a growing population of locally-adapted, mite-resistant bees. Instead, we were persuaded by the likes of Bayer that we should put pyrethroid-based miticides into our hives to kill off the foreign invaders. Within a few years - probably exacerbated by the simultaneous use of pyrethroids on much of the farmland of Britain - *Varroa* became immune to such treatment and we realized that far from solving the problem, we had made it worse by selecting for pyrethroid-resistant mites and the drug pushers had made a nice profit from the exercise.

It seems clear to me that while we continue to prop up our toxic food production system for the benefit of the agri-pharma-biotech industry, the fast-food merchants and the supermarkets, we will simply repeat the same ill-conceived, destructive cycles until we succeed in doing irreparable damage to our soil, our food supply and our planet. Given the apparent resistance of humans to learning repeated lessons, I am not optimistic about the future of the intrepid yet vulnerable *Apis mellifera* or that misnamed biped, mired in superstition, greed and self-interest: *Homo sapiens*.

Natural alternatives

When I wrote *The Barefoot Beekeeper* in 2007, I had no idea if anyone would listen or take me seriously, so it was with some surprise that I saw membership of the Natural Beekeeping Forum go from a handful, to a few hundred and quickly into the thousands, while my book sold more copies than I ever expected.

Emails told me that I had indeed tuned in to an unsuspected *zeitgeist*: 'natural beekeeping' was proving to be just what people had been looking for. Some were attracted by the low cost and simplicity of top bar hives, which enabled the bees to take charge of their homes once again and which required no heavy lifting and no extra equipment. Other long-term top-bar enthusiasts, mostly in the USA, found themselves being sought out by people who had never before considered keeping bees, but whose interest had been piqued by this low-tech, low-cost approach. Women, especially, who had felt pushed out of beekeeping by its male-dominated priesthood and their emphasis on production rather than nurture, began to return.

A movement was born.

The need for agricultural reform

However many of them there are, 'natural beekeepers' cannot hope to solve the bigger problem of a dysfunctional agricultural system. However, we share many values with organic growers, permaculture enthusiasts, homesteaders and those for whom nurturing healthy soil is a fundamental principle. We also have massive and largely untapped potential support among the general population, who need to hear the truth about what is being perpetrated on our land in the name of 'progress'.

If we and the bees are to have a shared future, we have a responsibility to help upcoming generations to rediscover their deep connection to the natural world - perhaps in some form of land-based education, such as 'farm-and-forest' schools - and thereby to redeem our collective failure to wrest control of our food production system from the hands of the power-hungry few.

So, while beekeeping is not - in the truest sense - 'natural', we do have a unique opportunity to learn from the bees, and through them, from the rest of the natural world. If we can direct our best minds towards developing a deeper understanding of the subtle and complex processes at work within multi-species eco-systems, we may - just possibly - be able to save ourselves from the dire fate that seems increasingly inevitable.

Balanced Beekeeping

Whatever accommodation we offer them, our meetings with bees have always been a process of negotiation, albeit somewhat one-sided. We can protect ourselves from them, but they ultimately have no protection from us. The encroachment of chemical agriculture, deforestation and urbanization have reduced their natural habitat, while toxic cocktails of insecticides have poisoned their flowers.

The honeybee has come to be seen as the 'canary in the coal mine' of our civilization and she is showing warning signs of her imminent demise, to which we must pay urgent attention.

Our challenge now is to re-negotiate our relationship with bees: we must learn to protect and nurture them, rather than simply exploit them, and we need to learn to listen to what they need from us. The process of discovering how we can most effectively do that is the project that myself and others have set ourselves, and we hope that many more will join us and carry this work forward. We acknowledge the paradox inherent in the phrase 'natural beekeeping': as soon as we consider 'keeping' bees, we begin to stray from what is truly 'natural'.

So our beekeeping practice must take into account:

- the natural impulses and behaviour of bees, including - foraging, swarming, storing food and defending their nest
- how hive design affects bee behaviour
- the suitability of materials used in hive construction
- the nature and frequency of our interventions

- the impact of a localized increase in honeybee population on other pollinators
- the balance between taking honey and leaving enough for the bees
- the effects of any disruptions to the brood nest

Conventional beekeepers tend to focus exclusively on honeybees, while those who take a more balanced approach consider it important to give some attention to the welfare of other species, especially bumblebees, mason bees and other solitary bees. It is not difficult to make wild bee conservation boxes, or you can provide more informal accommodation for them simply by making suitable habitat in your garden, using material such as rotting wood and leaves stacked in a corner, with some rudimentary protection from the worst of the weather.

We are engaged in a process of working towards the ultimately unattainable and paradoxical notion of completely 'natural' beekeeping, while acknowledging that the bees will go their own way regardless of our wishes. Our relationship with them is that of facilitator or minder rather than 'keeper'. We could say that the role of the natural beekeeper is to enable our bees to attain the fullest possible expression of their 'bee-ness' while in our care.

Our overall goal is to achieve a state of sustainability: balancing inputs and outputs such that - if possible - our activities enhance rather than damage the health of our bees, other species and the planet. To be truly sustainable, a system must close to carbon-neutral, requiring no synthetic inputs and having no detrimental impact on the natural environment.

Wasting energy

We have to consider what impact current

beekeeping practices have and how our 'natural' approach seeks to improve on this state of affairs.

A typical commercial beekeeping operation is a real energy hog. Lumber – which may or may not come from sustainable sources – is sliced and milled by powered machinery prior to assembly into hive boxes, which are transported by road, sea or rail to be further distributed by road to their apiary sites. Regular visits by beekeepers require oil-derived fuel, and more is needed to fire the boilers to heat the considerable quantities of water needed for sterilizing woodwork and washing down de-cappers, extractors, tanks and floors. More power is needed to retrieve the crop, to extract it and to mix and distribute the sugar syrup needed for the bees' survival following the removal of their stores. Honey must then be filtered, bottled and distributed to wholesalers and thence to retail outlets. Meanwhile, beeswax is recovered by means of steam or boiling water, cleaned and filtered and sent off to be re-melted and turned into sheets of foundation, which are then sold back to the beekeepers for insertion into frames for next season.

Migratory beekeepers in the USA truck hives by the thousands clear across the country for the almond pollination, and back across to Maine for the blueberries. In the UK this type of activity is nowadays largely restricted to taking hives up to the moors in August for the heather crop, and some orchard pollination work.

Due to what might be called the Langstroth hegemony, this whole scenario is also enacted in miniature by amateur beekeepers, who largely mimic the activities of their commercial brethren. They may only have a few hives at the bottom of their gardens, but in most cases they have not considered any alternative to the expensive, energy-hungry equipment available from the glossy catalogues of the beekeepers' suppliers.

We know that bees need nothing much more than a dry, ventilated cavity in which to build their nest. Instead, 'modern' beekeepers insist on supplying them with a box full of wooden frames, in which are mounted sheets of wax, helpfully imprinted with oversized 'worker-bee' hexagonal cell bases. A newly-hived swarm of bees must be surprised indeed to find so much done for them: ready-made comb bases hung in neat rows, with spaces all around them for access – what a boon for a busy colony!

Natural comb

But what may at first sight appear to be a great convenience, also has some significant drawbacks. All these imprinted cells are the same size, yet anyone who has observed natural comb knows that cell sizes vary considerably, and not just between workers and drones: worker cells themselves vary in diameter according to rules only bees are aware of. All those dead-straight frames may look neat, but bees don't build dead-straight comb – they like a gentle curve here and there. And if you watch bees building natural comb in an unrestricted space, they hang in chains, legs linked, as if laying out the dimensions of the comb in space as they work above their own heads – something they cannot do on foundation. The spacing between frames may also not be as they would choose, being arranged for the optimum production of workers, rather than the equally important drones.

So a good deal of so-called 'modern' beekeeping – in fact, virtually unchanged since the mid-19th century – is unsustainable from our point of view, as well as being a nuisance to bees. In terms of the beekeepers' honey yield, it is clearly an improvement on logs and skeps, but in terms of bee health, it has turned out to be a disaster.

The job of the natural beekeeper is to find ways of interacting with bees that are truly sustainable, both for the bees themselves and for the planet.

Principle-centred beekeeping

In *The Barefoot Beekeeper*, I proposed the following three, simple principles for the 'natural' beekeeper to consider:

- Interference in the natural lives of the bees is kept to a minimum.
- Nothing is put into the hive that is known to be, or likely to be harmful either to the bees, to us or to the wider environment and nothing is taken out that the bees cannot afford to lose.
- The bees know what they are doing: our job is to listen to them and provide the optimum conditions for their well-being, both inside and outside the hive.

These principles seem to me to form a solid foundation for our thinking. As soon as we step beyond those basic principles and attempt further to define the parameters, we find ourselves in danger of beginning to create a 'book of rules'. And it doesn't take much looking around the world today to see how divisive and destructive other 'books of rules' have been.

Balance

Like the honeybee colony itself, balanced beekeeping is a process, not a destination. We have to remain flexible and always be on the lookout for ways to sharpen our observational powers and improve our techniques. Everything I write and teach is offered in this spirit: here are some indications of what seems to work, always with the possibility that there are even better ways yet to be discovered, or – more likely – re-discovered, as there is really nothing new in beekeeping.

Historically, we began our relationship with bees when somebody discovered that the taste of honey was worth the pain it cost to harvest. We became honey-hunters; and while there were few of us and many of them, this was sustainable.

When somebody discovered that it was possible to offer shelter to honeybees while they made their honey, and then kill them off to raid their stores, we became bee keepers, and while there were few bee keepers and many honeybees, that too was sustainable.

Then someone invented a way to house bees that did not require them to be killed, but instead allowed people to manage and control them to some extent, tricking them into producing more honey for their masters than for themselves, and we became bee farmers. And that was sustainable for a while because there were still many of them and although there were also many of us, we could manipulate their reproduction so as to make more of them as we needed.

Now it has become clear that we have gone too far, for bees have begun to suffer from diseases that were virtually unknown in the old days, and they have to be given medicines in order to keep them alive. And because a whole industry has grown up around the farming of bees and there is a lot of money at stake, beekeepers have been slow to change their ways and many could not do so for fear of bankruptcy. So the health of honeybees has become worse and they are subject to parasites and viruses that never troubled them in the past.

Meanwhile, we forgot how to grow food in the way that we once had done because we were no longer inclined to labour in the fields, but instead devised clever ways to make the soil support more crops and farmed with machines. We poured fertilizers onto our fields and killed off inconvenient creatures with 'pesticides' – defining a whole class of living organisms as our enemies and therefore dispensable. This was never sustainable, and never can be.

That is where we find ourselves today, and this is the problem we face: bees have become weakened through exploitation and a toxic agricultural system, allied to the impossible expectation of continuous economic growth.

Nurturing bees

It seems to me that our most pressing work is to restore bees to their original, healthy state. We may think of ourselves as 'keepers' in the sense of 'nurturing and supporting' rather than 'enslaving'. We must seek to protect and conserve the honeybee by working within their natural capacity, not constantly urging them towards ever-greater production. We must challenge the whole agricultural and economic system that has caused us to arrive at this point, because without change at that level, the future for both us and the bees is bleak.

We can make a start by re-establishing more balanced and less violent ways of working with bees: neither we nor they have any need of routine or prophylactic 'treatments' with synthetic antibiotics, fungicides or miticides. We don't need to operate 'honey factories' – we can content ourselves with providing accommodation for bees in return for whatever they can afford to give us. In some years, this may be nothing at all, while in others there may be an abundant harvest.

Such is nature: bees depend on honey for their survival; we do not. And if the price of returning bees to a state of natural, robust health is a little less honey on our toast, is it not a worthwhile sacrifice?

The Importance of Drones

Drones have always had a bad press. Regarded as lazy and for the most part superfluous, they have been largely ignored, suppressed and sidelined by beekeepers. Even their name is synonymous with the more feckless and wasteful elements of humanity. I think it is time to restore them to their rightful place at the centre of colony activities and the focus of the queen's intention of reproducing her kind.

While 'natural beekeepers' are used to thinking of a honeybee colony more in terms of its intrinsic value to the natural world than its capacity to produce honey for human use, conventional beekeepers and the public at large are much more likely to associate honeybees with honey. This has, after all, been the main cause of the attention given to *Apis mellifera* since we began our association with them just a few thousand years ago.

In other words, I suspect most people - if they think of it at all - tend to think of a honeybee colony as 'a living system that produces honey'. We can safely assume that the bees themselves have another point of view.

The honeybee has evolved over millennia into the highly efficient, extraordinarily adaptable creature that we see and meet with today. By means of a number of behavioural modifications, she ensured a high degree of genetic diversity within the *Apis* genus; one such being the propensity of the queen to mate at some distance from her hive, at flying speed and tree-top height, with a dozen or so male bees, which have themselves travelled considerable distances from their own colonies.

Hybrid vigour
Multiple mating with exotic strangers assures a degree of heterosis - or 'hybrid vigour' - and carries its own

mechanism of selection for the bees involved: only the stronger, fitter drones ever get to mate with a quick and agile virgin queen. Contrast this with the practice of artificial insemination, routinely used by commercial breeders to create line-bred queens, where drone selection is performed not by the rigorous process of natural selection, but by a 'man in a white coat'. To add further insult to injury, it is common practice to replace AI queens each year, in the knowledge that they do not remain productive for nearly as long as their naturally-mated sisters, who have been recorded as living for six years or more.

Parthenogenesis

Another unusual feature of the honeybee is that the male bee - the drone - is born from an unfertilized egg; a process known as parthenogenesis. This means that the drones are haploid, i.e. have only one set of chromosomes, derived solely from their mother, because they themselves have no father. Her diploid (having two sets of chromosomes) daughters cannot reproduce and are thus a genetic dead end, which means that, in evolutionary terms, the queen's all-important biological imperative - to pass on her genes to future generations - is most clearly expressed in her sons, the drones.

So from an evolutionary point of view, the honeybee colony could be described as *'a living system for producing healthy, fertile drones for the purpose of perpetuating the species by spreading the genes of the best quality queens'*.

Thinking through this model of the honeybee colony gives us an entirely different perspective, when compared with the conventional view. We can now see nectar, honey and pollen as fuels for this system and the worker bees as servicing the needs of the queen, nurturing her babies by proxy and performing all the tasks required to ensure the smooth running of the colony, with the ultimate purpose of producing drones, which will carry the genes of their mother to virgin queens from other colonies far away.

We can speculate as to the environmental and biological triggers that cause drones to be raised at certain times and killed off at other times. We can consider the delicate mechanisms that may control the numbers of drones as a proportion of the overall population and define what other functions they may have inside the hive. We can only imagine how drones may be able to find their way to 'congregation areas', where they seem to gather when waiting for virgin queens to pass by, when they themselves rarely survive more than three months and hardly ever live through the winter.

There is much that we still do not know and may never fully understand.

Drone suppression

An important aspect of this way of looking at the honeybee colony is that it calls into question many of the practises of 'modern beekeeping' - by which I mean conventional, Langstroth-style, post-1850 beekeeping - which has always been focused on honey production above all else. From the point of view of our evolutionary model, many modern practises have been implemented with the *specific objective* of suppressing the raising of drones, thus running directly counter to the evolutionary interests of the queens.

In support of this thesis, we can cite the invention of wax foundation, impressed with the cell pattern of worker bees, deployed with the specific purpose of encouraging the colony to raise the maximum number of workers and the minimum number of drones. We can also lay some blame at the door of those who decided that frames should be spaced close together, allowing space only for the building of worker cells and forcing drone cells to the outer fringes of the comb. More recently, we can mention and condemn the encouragement from certain quarters to 'cull' drone pupae with the intention of reducing the population of *Varroa destructor* in our hives.

The history of modern beekeeping is replete with examples of anti-drone behaviour by beekeepers, from ignorance of their true role in the colony and in direct contradiction of the needs and instincts of the honeybee queen. Conventional beekeepers, however much they may protest their love and devotion for their charges, are in fact negating the wishes of their queen bees by focusing their efforts on the fuel of this intricate system, rather than the true purpose of the bee super-organism: the production of drones, without which *Apis mellifera* is doomed as certainly as the dinosaurs.

So 'natural beekeepers', with their focus on creating close-to-ideal environments for the use of honeybees and working in alignment with the desires of their queens are best placed to assure the future of the species. By raising healthy bees and allowing them to make as many drones as they wish, we can help to replenish the dearth artificially created by modern beekeeping methods.

And if some conventional beekeepers thank us for helping to improve their success rate for open queen mating, so much the better.

Do You Really Want to Keep Bees?

If you grow top fruit, beans, almonds, coppiced hazel or willow, flowering crops of any kind, or just have plenty of wild flowers in your garden, you will already have bees as visitors, so keeping a hive or two of honeybees would seem like a great idea. However, while my own main interest is in honeybees, my first piece of advice to gardeners thinking of taking up beekeeping is first to spend some time addressing the needs of other wild pollinators, especially bumblebees and solitary bees.

It may seem romantic to have thousands of honeybees buzzing round your flower beds, but the reality is that this picture is not entirely without problems. If your garden is small and urban, you may need to think carefully before placing a box of fifty thousand insects equipped with stings close to a neighbour's territory. There may be pets, children and elderly people to consider. You may want to think about how you use the space in your garden and how your activities - such as sunbathing, eating *al fresco* or simply hanging out the washing - may interfere with their flight-path, which at times may make Heathrow look like a quiet backwater.

I say these things not to put you off, but to encourage you to think carefully about what your real reasons for wanting to 'keep' bees may be.

The chances are that the flowering plants you grow are already being pollinated quite effectively by wild bees and other insects and unless you grow such crops on a large scale, adding honeybees to the mix will have only a marginal effect on yields. Exceptions to this might include areas where neighbours routinely spray with insecticides - with the result that wild insect numbers have been drastically reduced - or places where wild bee populations have suffered for other reasons, such as heavy pollution or habitat loss. Unfortunately, in such cases, you are probably in the wrong place to keep honeybees.

Management

Compared to most livestock, honeybees need little attention, and so can be added to a garden, homestead or smallholding without fear of creating a serious drain on your time. However, as with any other creature that comes within our care, someone must give them the right kind of attention at the right times, if only to ensure that they are comfortable, replete with stores and disease-free. Honeybees are - and will always remain - wild creatures, unimpressed by our attempts to domesticate them, so 'keeping' them is really a matter of providing suitable accommodation and allowing them freedom to roam. Beyond that - especially if you have honey in mind - you have to consider the degree and style of 'management' you will endeavour to apply.

Addressing the needs of other native bees first will help ensure that you do not cause an imbalance by flooding the area with honeybees while the local wild bee population is less than optimal. Exactly how this can be assessed is yet to be fully established, but if bumblebees are currently rare visitors to your garden, it may be too soon to add a beehive.

One of the most important considerations is the availability of food throughout the bees' flying season, and this is where the gardener can apply their particular skills to ensuring an appropriate variety of species. There is considerable overlap in the flower varieties visited by different types of pollinating insect and they each have particular preferences. For example, comfrey, red clover and foxglove tend to be preferred by bumblebees, while honeybees are more likely to be found on heathers, white clover and apple blossoms. Of the 'imported' species, Buddleia is famously attractive to butterflies, moths and many bee species, and Himalayan balsam provides a welcome late-season boost, despite the protests of some conservationists.

The honey trap

Of course, many - if not most - putative beekeepers are tempted in that direction by the prospect of having their own honey 'on tap'.

Honey yields are dependent on three main factors: the number of colonies kept, the extent and variety of available food and - more than anything - the weather. Of these, only the first is fully under your control, as bees may forage over a three mile (5 km) radius from their hive. If most of that territory is flower-rich meadows and hedgerows, organic farmland or verdant, uncultivated wild countryside, you are probably well placed to keep a dozen hives if you so choose.

Increasingly, beekeepers in towns and cities are finding their bees are healthier and more productive than those kept near arable farmland. The explanation for this seems clear: our agricultural system is a massive consumer of pesticides, fundicides and herbicides, which are known to be dangerous to pollinators. Much attention has lately been focused on the insidious destructive power of systemic neonicotinoids, including Imidacloprid, Clothianidin and Thiamethoxam, which are known to be highly toxic to bees in laboratory conditions, yet have been licensed for use in the field. They are typically applied as seed coatings, finding their way into the cellular structure of the plants as they grow and rendering the entire plant - from its roots to its pollen and nectar - toxic to anything that comes too close. Concern has also been expressed about their potential for toxicity to humans.

Choosing a hive

If you decide that you do want to bring honeybees into your life, an early choice you have to make is between 'conventional' beekeeping, using variations of the Langstroth-style frames-and-foundation hive, and so-called 'natural' beekeeping, which is mostly based on variants of the top bar hive. The route you follow will depend on your philosophy, your priorities and your pocket. The conventional approach requires a substantial initial investment in equipment, an ongoing dependence on bought-in supplies and the possibility of higher honey yields; while the natural path can be followed at a minimal cost, with generally lower but more sustainable yields and a low carbon footprint.

I suggest that before choosing your beekeeping path, you should first seek out opportunities to have some direct, hands-on encounters with live honeybees *en masse*. Not everyone is temperamentally suited to working with bees, and it is as well to establish this one way or the other before you find yourself with tens of thousands of them in your back yard.

Natural balance

There are some things all gardeners can do to help all bees and other pollinators, short of taking up bee keeping. The most important is to learn how to control pests using biological methods that do not require the use of toxic chemicals. Around 98% of all insects are beneficial to us in some way, but insecticides do not discriminate between 'friend' and 'foe'.

The next most important is to improve habitat by planting native, wild flowers - the kind that bees evolved with. There are lists of bee-friendly plants available online and there are some plant nurseries that specialize in them.

If you have space in your garden, letting some of it go wild to create a safe haven for bees and other insects is a great idea. Gardens that are too tidy are not so wildlife-friendly. Small piles of twigs and leaves and heaps of rocks are useful to many species.

Aside from the practical reasons why you may be considering keeping honeybees, they are undoubtedly an engaging species from which we have much to learn. Beekeeping is a fascinating and absorbing activity that has the potential to enrich your relationship with the landscape and its untamed inhabitants. And simply having more bees of all kinds around can add greatly to your enjoyment of your garden.

The Beatrix Potter Syndrome

When trying to understand something new, we look for parallels within our own experience: we automatically seek examples of something familiar in order – we imagine – the better to understand the unfamiliar. Often, this can be helpful, as when we learn a new language and we draw from our knowledge of another language with a common root. Unfortunately, our need to understand the unfamiliar in the light of the familiar can take us down a path that leads not to greater understanding, but to the confusion of fact with conditioned thought and to a form of distorted vision.

A favourite subject of this phenomenon is the interpretation of animal behaviour by reference to human behaviour, which we call anthropomorphism. Myths, fables and children's tales are so suffused with the granting of human values and character traits to animals that it is hard to think of a creature that has not, in our imaginations, been stereotyped and imprinted with characteristics ascribed to it by someone with an axe to grind. The fox is 'wily and cunning'; the dog is 'faithful and obedient'; the elephant is a 'gentle giant' and the snake is 'sneaky and deceitful'. Aesop probably started the trend, but I prefer to call it the 'Beatrix Potter Syndrome', in recognition of her influence on the developing minds of 20th century children, of whom I was one.

Beatrix Potter was an accomplished illustrator and observer of nature, who, had she been born a century later, may well have had a distinguished career in science. Sadly, she is now only remembered for her children's books depicting animals in human clothing, who walk upright on their hind legs. From her stories, a direct line can be drawn to the sentimental, emotionally charged portrayals of animals in Disney films.

Potter's assignation of human attributes and behaviour to animals is one form of anthropomorphism. There are at least two other ways in which we routinely corrupt our understanding of the non-human world by our use of language: the use of words to name or describe an animal, and the description of animal behaviour in human terms. Examples can be drawn from the world of bees to illustrate both of these phenomena.

So has anthropomorphism, anthropocentrism, sentimentality and mysticism distorted our relationship with bees?

Labels

When we label the egg-laying mother of the colony as 'queen' bee, we impose upon her by implication all the attributes with which that word is loaded. Thus we may expect to find her as a monarch in charge of the colony, issuing orders and, perhaps, punishments for infringements of 'colony law'. The term has passed back into the English language as a description of a woman with a controlling and manipulate nature, who likes to have people around her to serve her needs and give her attention. This reinforces the popular but inappropriate picture of a real queen bee, which should really be more accurately thought of as the egg-laying slave of the colony and certainly not its ruler. While the queen bee does indeed have a retinue of attendants to feed and groom her, it is they who lead her around and prepare places for her to lay. When she begins to show signs of a decline in her ability to provide eggs, she will be superseded and left to starve.

Likewise the drone, which has inherited the popular meaning of its name as a parasitic loafer, or one who lives off the labours of others. While the male bee does no obvious and visible work when compared with his sisters, we know remarkably little about their day-to-day activities due to the comparatively small amount of research that has been conducted on drones. I think it is highly improbable that a colony would deliberately encumber itself with a 'useless' 10-15% of its population at a time when gathering food is its primary concern. Simply because it is beyond our wit or our current technology to study them with due care does not entitle us to label them as 'surplus to requirements', which is how they are regarded by most conventional beekeepers. In fact, research by Juergen Tautz at Wurtzburg University has shown that drones do indeed have duties within the hive, and may well have functions outside that have so far eluded detection. As long ago as 1852, Moses Quinby suggested that drones would likely have functions in the hive beyond mating with a queen.

When we come to bee behaviour, so much of it is alien to us that we struggle to make sense of it, so it is not surprising that we resort to attempts to explain aspects of their world in human terms. We talk freely of bees gathering food, scouting for a nest site, defending their home, mating and carrying out their dead because these are all activities that we can easily relate to our own lives and make practical sense in terms of the day-to-day survival of any species.

Mysticism

What is perhaps more surprising – and infinitely less helpful – is when people concoct mystical 'explanations' derived entirely from their imaginations and pass them on as if they had some scientific validity. Possibly the worst offender in this respect in modern times is Rudolf Steiner, whose flights of fancy concerning bees bear not the slightest resemblance to observable reality, yet are regarded by his devotees as something close to holy writ, and thus beyond question. In his eight lectures on bees, delivered in November and December of 1923, Steiner sought to interpret the world of bees by means of his own-brand, Christianized version of a mystical 19th century cult known as 'theosophy', which he called 'anthroposophy'.

Steiner believed that mankind had existed on Earth - although not necessarily in material form - since its creation, and that bees (as well as other animals) were created for our benefit. This chronological reversal of the truth as revealed by fossil evidence - bees having certainly been around for more than 100 million years before *Homo sapiens* - sets the scene for further dubious assertions, such as when he talks of embryonic queens "giving off light" that somehow causes a colony to swarm from "fear that it no longer possesses the bee poison".

Anyone unfamiliar with Steiner's idiosyncratic cosmology and his other writings about the supposed history of the Earth may be surprised by passages such as:

> *"Our earth was once in a condition of which one could say that it was surrounded by clouds that had plant-life within them; from the periphery, other clouds approached and fertilised them; these clouds had an animal nature. From cosmic spaces came the animal nature; from the earth the essence of plant-being rose upwards."* (Lecture VIII)

Back in the world of bees, Steiner makes much of the 21-day gestation period of a worker bee as being equivalent to *"a single rotation of the sun on its axis"* (Lecture II), apparently unaware that the equatorial regions of the sun perform a single rotation in 25.6 days, while polar regions rotate once in about 36 days (NASA).

He goes on to say that *"the drone is thus an earthly being"* (because its completion takes longer than the sun's rotation - which in fact, as we now know, it does not).

He further elaborates on this thesis:

> "The drones are the males; they can fertilize; this power of fertilization comes from the earth; the drones acquire it in the few days during which they continue their growth within the earth-evolution and before they reach maturity. So we can now say: in the bees it is clearly to be seen that fertilization (male fecundation) comes from the earthly forces, and the female capacity to develop the egg comes from the forces of the Sun. So you see, you can easily imagine how significant is the length of time during which a creature develops. This is very important for, naturally, something happens within a definite time which could not occur in either a shorter or a longer time, for then quite other things would happen."

As happens a number of times in the Lectures, Steiner makes a statement that is demonstrably erroneous, and then goes on to elaborate a specious argument from it, which, being derived from false premises, must inevitably lead to false conclusions.

It would be tedious to cite every instance where Steiner is obfuscatory, unnecessarily mystical or just plain wrong. Suffice to say that, while not being totally devoid of interest, his Lectures are about as useful a source of insights into bees as a medieval book of medicinal herbs would be for conducting modern surgery. Indeed, Steiner even betrays his lack of basic understanding of the functions of the human body (Lecture VII) in saying that:

> "... It is represented as though the heart were a kind of pump, and that this pumping of the heart sends the blood all over the body. This is nonsense, because it

> *is in reality the blood which is brought into motion by the ego-organization, and moves throughout the body."*

However, Steiner does make some non-mystical statements that must be considered, as they at least fall into alignment with observable reality. He warns against pushing bees for over-production, drawing a parallel with the dairy industry (Lecture V); he emphasizes that *"... The bee-colony is a totality. It must be seen as a totality."* (Lecture V); The one much-vaunted but often misquoted 'prediction' made by Steiner, usually misrepresented as a 'prophesy' of the general demise of bees, amounts to a rather mild criticism of the then relatively new practice of artificial insemination: *"...we must see how things will be in fifty to eighty years time...".*

Right at the end of the final Lecture, we find clear evidence that Steiner's view of nature is actually highly anthropocentric:

> *"Thus we can say: When we observe things in the right way, we see how the processes of Nature are actually images and symbols of what happens in human life. These men of olden times watched the birds on the juniper trees with the same love with which we look at the little cakes and gifts on the Christmas tree."... I have therefore spoken of the juniper tree which can truly be regarded as a kind of Christmas tree, and which is the same for the birds as the blossoms for the bees, the wood for the ants, and for the wood-bees and insects in general."*

And so Steiner's mysticism, as well as his sentimentality, turns out to have a large component of anthropomorphism lurking within it.

The Zen of beekeeping

Having reached this point, we have to consider what is left: what would be a legitimate methodology for the study of bees, that would be free from the elephant traps of anthropocentrism, anthropomorphism, sentimentality and mysticism, yet can encompass the sense experienced by many who come into contact with bees that there is 'something else' present, beyond the purely material?

A rationalist might say, *'observe without interpretation: see what is there and describe it as accurately as possible, but without overlaying it with meaning. Be true to observable reality'*.

And yet, many people report some kind of transcendental experience in the presence of bees, so are their reports to be written off as mere whimsy?

Speaking from my own experience, I can say that while working with bees and maintaining a calm, unhurried demeanour, I have had moments of inner peace akin to that I have also experienced while meditating or engaging in certain martial arts practices that aim to still the mind and sharpen awareness. Having one's unprotected hands in a hive of fully-armed bees has a way of focusing the mind very much in the moment, while any deviation from the 'now' is likely to be punished more rapidly and more severely than by a Zen master's staff.

Being truly present 'in the moment' is a rarer - and thus more precious - experience for 21st-century Internet-dwellers than for our ancestors. For the opportunity to experience that sense of timelessness in the company of a wild creature so many millennia our senior is a privilege that beekeepers should celebrate and cherish.

Mysticism has had its day. We are grown-ups now: we have seen the atom bomb and the double helix and we need to come to terms with the world and life in all its wonderful forms without ascribing all phenomena just beyond our understanding to the work of gods, aliens, faeries or gnomes. We can appreciate nature without projecting our aspirations or values onto it. We can observe without always needing to know the 'hidden meaning' of what we see hear, smell and taste. We can be elevated by what is around us and enjoy all the sensations available to us. We can even compose poems and songs, myths and fables to entertain us and our children, but we no longer need to sit at the feet of all-too-mortal men who exert power over the ignorant by interposing themselves between us and direct, authentic experience of the mysteries of life.

The Bigger Picture

More, perhaps, than any other order of animals on Earth, the *Hymenoptera* (bees, ants and wasps) have shaped our landscape and our diet, largely unnoticed and unacknowledged.

Until the industrial revolution, we were - broadly speaking - living in a state of dynamic balance with all other species; our own population being kept in check by plagues, epidemics and our predilection for inter-tribal warfare. Having since convinced ourselves that we are masters of the natural world - an extraordinarily arrogant delusion, rooted in religious dogma rather than common sense - we now seem to behave as if other life-forms exist merely to serve our need for food, leisure or entertainment.

By adopting and domesticating animals such as horses, dogs and cats, farming unnatural numbers of cattle and sheep, and turning urban areas into feeding grounds for foxes and badgers, we have grossly distorted the density of some species at the expense of others. Likewise in the arable countryside, we have covered swathes of it in a limited range of crops, inevitably attracting certain species we consequently regard as pests. We respond by applying insecticides and selective herbicides, which further distorts the picture by destroying a significant proportion of soil-dwelling species, including the vital and delicate fungal *micorrhiza*, which support all plant life and - by extension - all animal life.

Toxins

Meanwhile, honeybees have solved the problem faced by all wild animals - that of gathering and storing food - by simultaneously dividing and multiplying the body of their super-organism, creating a powerful and wide-ranging foraging force with the ability to gather, process and store more than its own weight in food every day. The down-side of their efficiency in a world dominated by humans is that they are uniquely vulnerable to the smallest change in the chemistry of flowers on which they depend. Any additive we apply to our crops - even in the tiniest quantities - will be gathered unwittingly and concentrated within the confines of their nest, where its effects will inevitably be magnified.

Of the 30,000 or so novel chemicals that have entered our environment since the middle of the 20th century, many are known to be or likely to be poisonous to bees. Some of the most toxic are relatively recent introductions: the neonicotinoids, which are currently the most widely-used class of systemic insecticides. The current ubiquity of these chemical weapons of mass insect destruction can be laid squarely at the door of Bayer, one of the most ruthless and unscrupulous of the 'Big Pharma' corporations, which between them effectively control the global, toxic industry that is modern agriculture.

Before any insecticide can be sold in the USA, it has to be approved by the so-called Environmental Protection Authority, which requires a certain amount of data from the manufacturer as part of the approval process. They do not, however, require independent or long-term testing: merely - it seems - the bare minimum to suggest that the proposed insecticide will not cause immediate and obvious problems to known and highly visible species. Because chemical manufacturers are always in a hurry to exploit the commercial potential of any new product, they employ professional lobbyists and make substantial contributions to political campaign funds to ensure that their interests are well-represented in the corridors of power.

Loophole

To make matters easier for the manufacturers, there is a handy loophole in the EPA regulations, which allows a product that has not yet gone through the full approval process to be marketed under a temporary licence. The effect of this is to enable the likes of Bayer - which has an appalling record of selling all manner of chemicals that were later 'discovered' to be far more toxic than was admitted to regulatory authorites - to sell billions of dollars-worth of potentially extremely dangerous, under-tested products virtually 'on the nod'. If, some years later, an independent researcher manages to conduct independent tests and finds it to be rather less 'safe' than claimed, it is just possible that they may persuade the EPA to revoke the licence, but this can be an extremely laborious and time-consuming process with a low chance of success, as the original manufacturer will fight it all the way with all the considerable resources at its disposal. And in the end, if the product is eventually pulled, vast profits will already have been banked and another - possibly even more toxic - range will be in the pipeline ready for another iteration of the largely illusory approval process.

The corruption of science

Pure science is the pursuit of knowledge for its own sake. The best scientists are those whose intense curiosity about life, the universe and everything leads them to devote their lives to the quest for truth; or as close to truth as human intellect and ingenuity can approach. As such, they represent all that is fine and admirable in the human spirit and deserve our recognition and respect far more, I would suggest, than the self-indulgent, attention-seeking actors and sporting heroes beloved of the popular media.

The problems start when you combine science with business and introduce the profit motive into the equation. Rather than being about broadening and deepening our knowledge, the game is driven by the marketing department and becomes focused on ways in which new knowledge can be exploited for profit. In the absence of an ethical underpinning, this is a recipe for disaster on an unprecedented scale.

My science education - such as it was - conditioned my thinking very much along materialistic, mechanistic lines. Compound A added to compound B always produces compound C; objects under this set of conditions always behave in this fashion; planets rotate and orbit in regular, predictable ways and most phenomena have particular, logical explanations. The fact that much of what was thought of as 'scientific fact' 500 years ago is now considered worthy only of scorn and derision, was glossed over and explained only in terms of 'progress' and the improvement of scientific method over the intervening years.

The big picture

If you are in any way surprised or shocked by this, you really should be: the well-being of our planet and our children's future is being eroded by manipulative, profit-driven psychopaths in suits, whose arrogance towards and extraordinary ignorance of natural processes have caused a massive upset in the dynamic equilibrium of nature, the longer-term effects of which may yet seal our fate.

Of course, there is a possibility that I am over-stating my case: that I am arrogantly imposing my beliefs onto an essentially harmless scenario and that the scientists in the pay of 'Big Pharma' know exactly what they are doing and are working solely for the benefit of the natural world and the health of humankind. But on the balance of probabilities, given that profit is the sole driving force behind these unimaginably huge corporate entities, and given their proven capacity for the destruction of human life, up to and including genocide, I suspect that, if anything, I err on the side of understatement.

It seems to me that those of us who see the big picture - however out-of-focus it sometimes may be - have a duty to communicate as best we can the potential dangers we see ahead if the relentless wheel of 'progress' is allowed to turn unchecked. To fail to do so would be to fail our children and our children's children, who may otherwise legitimately ask, *"If you could see what was happening, why didn't you do something about it?"*

Sustaining the Honeybee

The big lesson of the 20th century was this: the way we treat the natural world has repercussions way beyond the immediately obvious. Our destruction of rain forests and other habitats in the name of 'progress' has triggered irrevocable, cumulative cycles of species loss, soil erosion and climate change that we are only just beginning to understand and that will haunt us for generations.

From here, we can look back over the last 150 years and see how commercial beekeeping developed from the Victorian desire to dominate the natural world and subjugate its inhabitants to the will of man. This was the dominant paradigm throughout the first two thirds of the twentieth century, until we began to wake up to what was happening to the planet as a result of our arrogant assumption that we could treat it as a bottomless waste pit.

Some of us looked out at decimated forests, depleted soil and polluted water and realized that we had collectively to change our ways. In my case, the moment of epiphany came in 1971, when Edward Goldsmith gave a lecture at my college about the background to the imminent publication of his new magazine, The Ecologist. Shortly afterwards, new organizations, such as Friends of the Earth and Greenpeace, sprung up to lead an awakening generation and the anti-M3 protests began around Winchester in Hampshire, in an ultimately doomed yet inspired effort to save a valued tract of chalkland meadow from the encroachment of what we were told was 'progress'.

The subsequent growth of the organic food movement indicates the beginnings of a shift in human perception, while the global dominance of a handful of corporations, intent on covering the earth with their genetically mutated organisms and chemical-dependent crops, represents the old order, stubbornly clinging to outmoded, reductionist science as their gospel and taking their moral guidance and business model from drug pushers.

So it is with the bees. Since Langstroth introduced us to the wonders of his movable-frame hive, we have assumed that we know better than they do what living conditions they require, what size cells they prefer to build, how many colonies can live in close proximity - and every other detail of their lives down to the mating of their queens, we have sought to bring under our control. And now we are reaping the rewards of our arrogance: bees that are dependent for their survival on chemical inputs and human interventions, and which abandon their hives in growing numbers.

Cell size

Can this situation be reversed? Nobody can say for sure, but those of us who are experimenting with sustainable beekeeping systems believe that the answer lies in a low-tech, low-impact approach, that allows bees to build comb according to their own design, eliminating the artificial constraints imposed on them by the use of frames and foundation.

Foundation - thin sheets of wax impressed with the beginnings of hexagonal cells - was introduced as a way of 'helping' the bees; saving them some work and therefore redirecting their energy towards doing more work for us, i.e. making more honey. Because it is milled to what has been decreed is the 'correct' cell size for worker bees, then that is what the bees are more-or-less forced to build. Because the generally adopted cell size of worker foundation is 0.3-0.5mm larger than those that feral bees build unaided, this may have led to an overall increase in the size of the bees themselves, due to the fact that they grow to the capacity of the cells in which they pupate.

Larger bees were thought to be a good thing, as they would surely have longer probosces, thus enabling them to feed on formerly unreachable nectars, plus a larger payload capacity for nectar and pollen. Unfortunately, enlargement appears also to have resulted in reduced flying efficiency, shorter lifespan and quite possibly an increased susceptibility to disease and parasites.

Proponents of 'small-cell' foundation claim that a significant decrease in the *Varroa* population results from its use, due - it is suggested - to there being less space in the cells for them to reproduce, combined with a roughly one-day reduction in the worker bee emergence date compared with 'large-cell' bees. But this is still a step short of full 'naturalization'. The fact is that, given the choice, bees do not build uniform worker cells, but vary the size according to factors we can only guess at. Foundation or artificial comb - of whatever size - is part of the old 'we-know-best' paradigm that has caused their current problems. Having seen the beautifully formed, naturally constructed comb that bees build in skeps and in my top bar hives, I would not go back to frames and foundation if Thornes were giving them away.

Bees need to build comb. It is a part of their natural life-cycle and a part of their biochemical make-up to extrude wax and to work it, and they need the freedom to build it their way. If that means they raise 10%, 15% or even 20% of their colony as drones, then so be it: that is what they need to do and we may never know the reason why, nor do we need to. It would not surprise me if the many stories of poor quality queens I have heard and read about recently were caused by a local shortage of good drones.

Sustainability

It seems to me that beekeeping - especially commercial beekeeping - is no longer sustainable in its present form. We need to re-think our management methods from top to bottom, or face an unprecedented decline in the health and strength of the bee population and the end of honey - at least in the public perception - as a pure, healthy food.

Intensive beekeeping - especially on a commercial scale - generates massive amounts of time- and energy-consuming work in return for a variable and unpredictable honey crop. Copious quantities of power and water are consumed in manufacturing, cleaning and sterilizing equipment, rendering wax and cleaning up the inevitable, intractable, sticky mess. Transporting our kit around the countryside burns carbon fuels by the tankful. Substantial buildings are required for storing mountains of woodwork and housing de-capping machines, extractors, boilers, tanks and all the myriad bits and pieces that inevitably accumulate around a beekeeping operation. Hives, frames, supers, feeders and covers are manufactured using power-hungry, saws and planes, while human time and energy is spent nailing together bits of wood, fitting foundation and repairing broken parts.

Treatments

Meanwhile, 'scientific' chemical treatments have resulted in fitter parasites and tougher bacteria. We artificially maintain strains of bee that are ill-equipped to deal with infections or infestations, despite their ancestors having done so, unaided, for at least 100 million years. Some beekeepers routinely use potentially dangerous and illegal chemicals - including antibiotics and organo-phosphates - risking prosecution and loss of reputation, as well as their own and their customers' health, while making little or no long-term impact on the bees' problems. Many of these chemicals are lipophilic (fat-loving) and persist in wax, which is recycled into foundation and imparts a low-level dose of a cocktail of who-knows-what to the next generation of bees.

All this might be understandable if the consistent outcome was bumper crops of honey and happy, healthy bees. However, honey crops will forever depend more on the weather than any other single factor and, as I write, our bees are suffering from unprecedented levels of infestation by the *Varroa* mite and endemic infection by viruses for which mites are the most likely vector. Thanks to those who persist in shipping bees around the world instead of breeding from local stocks, the Small Hive Beetle and the *Tropilelaps* mite will most probably arrive in Britain soon. So-called Africanized bees may not be far behind.

In our modern, western world, where relatively few people have a day-to-day, intimate relationship with nature, public appreciation and understanding of the pivotal importance of the honeybee in the greater scheme of things has been largely lost. Bees are regarded by many as a pest rather than a vital, natural resource. A surprising number of people cannot tell a honeybee from a wasp, as many swarm catchers will testify. Our government, it seems, would rather cover the countryside with untested, genetically modified crops than invest in truly sustainable, organic farming or fund research into bee diseases. Even our British Bee Keepers Association has been taking money from agri-chemical companies in return for their patronage of bee-killing insecticides and passive acceptance of GM crops.

In practical terms, sustainability may mean accepting lower honey production per colony in return for healthier bees. It may mean - at least in the short term - accepting heavier winter losses in return for improved vigour in surviving colonies. It almost certainly means increased vigilance in inspecting colonies and assessing desirable traits, which will mean that more beekeepers will need to educate themselves beyond a basic level in bee husbandry and breeding, which can be no bad thing.

Remediation

The remedy, as well as the blame, for the current parlous state of beekeeping lies with beekeepers themselves: nobody else knows enough or cares enough to take the necessary action. We need to share more information with each other and make more effort to educate the public, especially the next generation. We may need to re-think much of what we now take for granted, even if it means discarding protocols we have regarded as holy writ for the last 150 years. We may have to think the unthinkable: that commercial-scale beekeeping is inherently unsustainable. After all, keeping 50 or 100 or more beehives in an area that nature might furnish with only one or two colonies is very like cramming 10,000 chickens into a battery farm and has similar implications for aberrant behaviour and spread of diseases.

For me, beekeeping is mostly a conservation and restoration project. Much as I love honey, I am more interested in breeding bees that can look after themselves. I don't know to what extent I will succeed, but since 2007, over 6000 people have joined our online forum and by freely sharing information, we are developing a balanced approach to not-for-profit beekeeping that shows signs of becoming genuinely sustainable.

Feedback

A key test of intelligence is the ability to adapt one's behaviour according to feedback from the environment. The feedback from the bees right now is surely telling us to change our ways or lose them forever, and thereby risk sealing our own fate. We must look more closely at our complicity in the over-use of agricultural chemicals and find better ways to achieve our goal of a fair honey crop than the propagation of poisons. We must accept that synthesized treatments for mites and brood diseases are ultimately doomed to failure, as they inevitably create dependency. The real answer lies with the bees themselves. Our job is to provide them with the best possible conditions in which they can solve their own problems, as they have always done.

Asking Questions

I think I must have been born skeptical. Others may use less kindly terms about me, but it has always been my habit to question everything stated as 'fact' by anyone in a position of authority. This inability - or unwillingness - to accept what I was told without good evidence must have been annoying to my parents and my teachers and I am quite sure that it has caused me to be less than popular with sales people, but it has taken me down some interesting paths. Recently, it has led me into the fascinating world of bees and thence towards a greater curiosity about and interest in the way our food is grown and processed.

Bees and other pollinators are, of course, very much involved in the production of food for humans; whether or not they are aware of this and whether they care one way or the other are avenues of philosophical speculation down which I choose not to travel.

The intelligence of bees

If we define intelligence as the ability to solve problems, then individual bees do not seem to possess much of it. This will become apparent if you watch a bee repeatedly trying to fly through a closed window rather than flying off in a different direction to test other possible escape routes.

Collectively, however, the honeybee colony is capable of solving the most complex problems of survival: where and how to build a home; how to defend against predators; how to find food and how to store it against periods of dearth. So somehow the honeybee super-organism possesses a degree of intelligence that appears to be greater than the sum of its parts.

This raises several interesting questions, such as:

- Is 'colony intelligence' proportional to the number of bees present, and therefore variable according to the season?
- If so, what are the implications for swarming, making splits, etc?
- Is there a threshold population below which 'colony intelligence' cannot be observed?
- What is the role of the queen in 'colony intelligence' and how is it affected by re-queening?
- Are packages, which have queens unrelated to the rest of the bees, less intelligent than colonies with their own queen?
- Does a colony generate an 'energy field' of some kind - perhaps something along the lines of Rupert Sheldrake's 'morphic field' - that provides a 'pattern' for their behaviour?

The consideration of such questions as these will add considerably to your appreciation of bees and how little we really know about them.

Bee-friendly bugs

One of the questions I began to ask myself early in my path of bee-discovery was, "What are the differences between a typical 'modern' bee hive and a hollow tree?"

The almost universal use of miticides over the last half century, together with a somewhat obsessive attitude towards sterilization of equipment, has turned conventionally-managed hives into bee mono-cultures, at the expense of a multitude of moulds, fungi, insects and arachnids whose functions and interactions in the wild we know virtually nothing about.

Keeping bees in isolation, in sterile boxes, has to me always been counter-intuitive, considering that no species in the natural world lives apart from all others and that hollow trees must teem with all manner of flora and fauna that is banished from the modern beehive by chemical or heat sterilization and the use of plastics. Only now we are discovering that some of these little bugs may well hold the secret of how pests and diseases are kept at bay in the natural home of bees; by a self-organizing, self-balancing, mutually-negotiated interaction of interdependent, living ingredients. For example, experiments with mites of the *Stratiolelaps* genus are proving their potential for controlling *Varroa* and I suspect that even the ubiquitous earwig and wood louse may have parts to play. At least one predatory mite, *Parasitellus focorum*, previously associated with bumblebees, is finding its way into the chemical-free hives of natural beekeepers and quite possibly doing its best to reduce the *Varroa* population. Who knows what other potentially useful functions it may have?

My own experiments in re-creating this in-hive ecosystem using what some people are calling the 'deep litter floor' are showing promising early results. The idea is to create an environment where other bee-friendly species can live and negotiate their relationship with bees as a designed-in feature of the hive, rather than leaving it to chance. My current iteration uses an extension to the floor of the hive, filled with wood shavings and seeded with 'floor sweepings' from the ground around the hive and some small pieces of rotting wood, which I hope will contain at least some of the desired species.

There is much potential for refinement of this idea and a proper assay of species typically found living with bees would certainly be useful, although I have a lot of faith in the tendency of ecosystems to find their own balance.

Meanwhile, let's continue to ask ourselves questions, such as, *"What else can we do to help the bees?"*

Advice to Inventive Beekeepers

Judging from my own experience (a.k.A.mistakes), as well as many posts from new beekeepers on our forum, the temptation for beginners to re-invent the wheel - or at least, the beehive - is almost overwhelming. Here are some notes intended not to discourage creativity, but to dampen the ardour of those tempted to proselytize too soon:

- Whatever clever little gizmo you dream up, it has probably been thought of and put through several iterations already. If you don't see it out there in daily use, it has most likely -

(a) been tried and found wanting, or

(b) been superseded by something better.

- Bees are amazingly versatile and adaptable and will happily live in a wide variety of containers of all shapes and many sizes. Just because they seem to enjoy living this year in your new hive, which you dreamed up one morning over coffee, does not necessarily mean that you have just invented The Perfect Bee Hive. Test your design for at least 3-5 years before making any public claims for it, and even then, be prepared for the bees to show a preference for something different next season.

- Keep It Simple. Please. Before installing any gadget or gizmo, ask yourself, "What problem does this solve?" If you have to hesitate before answering, you should probably abandon it there and then.

- Henry David Thoreau once said, "Beware of

any enterprise that requires new clothes, rather than a new wearer of clothes." Had he been a beekeeper, he could have said, "Beware of any beekeeping method that requires a new hive, rather than a new keeper of bees."

- Bees never lie and will always let you know their honest preferences in all things.
- Listen. Watch. Learn.

Inner Beekeeping

An aspect of our relationship with bees that has so far received relatively little attention is what we might call 'inner beekeeping', by which I mean the ways in which our contact with bees impinge on our understanding of ourselves and how this, in turn, affects the way we relate to other people and to the natural world. Learning about ourselves through the medium of bees, if you like.

Many writers have attempted to draw lessons in morality, social behaviour and even politics from their observations of bee colonies, but all those I have read fell headlong into the elephant trap of anthropomorphic projection: the tendency to see bees as 'little people' and to interpret their behaviour according to the moral, social and political prejudices of the author.

The areas that particularly interest me include:

- How working with bees can help us to overcome our primitive fears;

- How being around bees can influence our state of mind, and how this may feed back to influence the bees;

- What we can learn from our observations of bees that we may be able usefully to apply to our own lives, free from amthropomorphism, moral and political judgements.

Overcoming fear

With respect to bees, most normally-adjusted people (excluding beekeepers, that is) would, I think, be able to place themselves somewhere on a spectrum that had 'healthy wariness' at one end and 'naked phobia' at the other. Which is to say that some degree of fear is commonly associated with being in close proximity to creatures known to be capable of inflicting pain, ranging in severity from the merest pin-prick all the way through to anaphylaxis and - for the unlucky few - death.

Many people have told me that they were 'allergic' to bee stings, but on closer questioning their response was really no more than some itchy, localized swelling, which is the normal immune system response to the injection of a toxic irritant into the bloodstream. A real allergic response is likely to involve redness and swelling around the throat, leading to difficulty in breathing and unconsciousness. Any suggestion of such symptoms should be treated as a medical emergency.

Even without the danger of a truly allergic response, the immediate pain of a sting to someone not used to it is something of a shock and can cause some people to panic. Learning to override this reaction is a challenge that all novice beekeepers face, and failure to meet it is probably the most common reason for people giving up beekeeping in their first or second season.

One thing handling bees can teach us is that facing and overcoming fears is a part of the process of growing up that can continue throughout life. Consciously exposing oneself to the causes of fear and working through the feelings that arise is an act that requires a certain amount of courage, so approaching a bee colony for the first time is a challenge for many people. On the face of it, putting one's bare hands inside a box that is home to 50,000 insects, which, if they chose to, could collectively inject you with a potentially lethal dose of venom equivalent to a rattlesnake bite, is in the 'swimming with sharks' category of borderline insane behaviour.

So why do so many people consider it normal?

The nature of fear

We can start by looking at the nature of rational fear; a mechanism based partly on direct experience and partly on instinct, hard-wired into our mind-body that protects us from indulging in life-threatening activities, such as stepping too close to the edge of a cliff, or jumping into a raging torrent, or wandering unprotected into the territory of large, hungry carnivores. The fight-or-flight response is the manifestation of a primitive, fear-driven behaviour, which, by pumping adrenalin into our bloodstream, gives us an extra burst of energy that will often enable us to escape potentially dangerous situations that occur without warning. Such a behaviour has obvious survival value.

A phobia, on the other hand, is an irrational fear; typically the result of a single-event, childhood conditioning, focused on essentially harmless subjects such as spiders or public speaking.(Of course, there are places in the world where a fear of spiders is entirely rational, as well as places where saying certain things in public would put you in danger.) Phobias are capable of being generalized; so a fear of one type of insect may easily be transferred to another. Wasps, being, I think, generally more inclined to sting humans than bees are - possibly because of their barb-less stinger, which they can withdraw from our elastic skin without damage to themselves - are the subject of phobic responses by many people, who are likely to readily transfer this feeling to similar-looking bees, particularly if they cannot differentiate between the two.

We cannot say that a fear of the bee's sting is wholly irrational, as there may be a real danger of personal injury along with a guarantee of a certain amount of pain, from which we are biologically programmed to recoil. Such fear can be ameliorated by covering oneself in bee-proof clothing, as bees are limited by their size and physiology when it comes to attacking humans, so a well-fitting suit and leather gloves will keep them at bay if they turn nasty.

However, the real test of one's ability to overcome fear is to work with them wearing only the minimum of protection, as this will ensure that you stay alert and act in a way that is least likely to alarm them. After all, we can reasonably suppose that fear is also the primeval emotion in bees that can be triggered by a large, clumsy mammal in close proximity to their home.

Minimum protection

My preference, when working with bees, is to dispense with body armour and gloves and only to protect my head and face with a hat and veil, as a sting in the eye may cause blindness and stings anywhere on the face can be particularly painful.

It's not that I am immune to pain - far from it - but I have learned to tolerate it for the sake of being able to handle bees without harming them. I dislike wearing gloves because they dull my sense of touch - the vital channel that warns me, by means of a most delicate sensation on my fingers, the moment before I squash a bee. On occasions where I have been obliged to wear gloves or suffer a large number of stings, I have found that my sensitivity suffers and bees get squashed, resulting in more bees joining in the attack and exacerbating the situation. These days, my gloves are reserved for the handling of the occasional bad-tempered colony, and I encourage my students to go bare-handed as soon as they feel confident to do so. A drop or two of clove oil makes an invisible and for the most part quite effective pair of 'gloves' (a tip passed on to me by Peter Donovan, who learned his beekeeping directly from Brother Adam).

Approaching a hive

While fear is something to recognize and overcome, there is always a case for caution and due care. Bees should always be handled gently and with respect; only a fool takes the mood of a strong colony for granted. Fortunately, bees usually put a warning shot across our bows before unleashing their heavy artillery, although this may not be the case with the so-called 'Africanized' bees that are now endemic across central America and the southern states of the USA.

As I approach a hive, I watch what is going on at the entrance and note any tendency for bees to change course and check me out. Bees that are intent on their business and continue to behave as if I was not there are unlikely to resent a quick check behind the follower boards, while those who send out an advance guard to head-butt my veil and buzz around my head are to be treated with caution and may be telling me that they are unwilling to tolerate my presence at that time, in which case - unless I absolutely must carry out a particular operation - I quietly move away.

While working inside a hive, slow, smooth movements are desirable, with the utmost care being taken to avoid sudden knocks or jarring or other actions that may alarm bees. Any side attachments should be carefully freed with a sharp, flexible blade, before a comb is moved and care should be taken never to lift one comb while it is close to another, to avoid rolling bees over each other, which they hate.

Because top bar hives are always opened from one end at a time, it is possible to see a good deal of what is going on inside the hive without moving a single comb. If you do need to check further in than you can see, it is often possible to move combs such that little disturbance to their work occurs and sometimes they barely seem to notice you are there. This compares favourably with any other type of hive that I have seen or handled. Only a straw skep, rolled onto its back, gives as much information to the beekeeper with almost as little disturbance.

Learning From Bees

In attempting to draw lessons from the natural world, it is all too easy to fall into the trap of anthropomorphic projection. This has frequently been the case with observers of honeybees, who, simply by applying names – such as 'queen', 'drone' and 'worker' – have coloured our perception of the species such that it is difficult to approach a honeybee colony with a truly open mind. We have been led to expect to find a monarch in command of her myriad subjects, comprising workaholic females and lazy, good-for-nothing males. The truth is quite different: the bee we call 'queen' can more realistically be seen as an egg-laying servant to her offspring, who have perfected the arts of consensus decision-making and communal, co-operative living beyond anything we have achieved. They have subsumed individual egos to the super-organism and evolved a highly successful way to thrive in an ever-changing world, only recently coming under threat from the synthetic products of man's crude attempts to 'tame' nature by means of perverted science.

However, by observing the actual behaviour of honeybees, we may be able to identify some lessons we could usefully apply to our own lives.

Here are some examples of lessons we could learn from bees:

- Honeybees live within their means. There are no loans or credit cards in the bees' world; only the resources they themselves gather. Their 'bank' is their store of food, garnered when nature provides and stored for the times when foraging is not possible.Like us, bees need to eat every day, and they do everything in their power to ensure a constant food supply by storing it –

not so much for themselves, but for bees yet to be born.

- Honeybees achieve extraordinary things by working together. Fifty thousand workers can shift a lot of stuff. Co-operation is the key to their success: tens of thousands of individuals behaving as a single organism.

- Honeybees demonstrate that division of labour can be highly efficient; while everyone knowing how to do the full range of essential jobs makes for flexibility and adaptability. Bees move through a series of jobs in the hive before finally emerging as food-gatherers. In an emergency, they can revert to their former occupations to make up for losses.

- Honeybees make honey while the sun shines. Bees are opportunists, taking advantage of available food as soon as conditions are right. Even when their stores seem full, they will find odd corners to pack with food.

- Honeybees behave as though individuals matter, while the common good is always their first priority. Ego is not a feature of honeybees: their first duty is to their family and bees will sacrifice themselves without hesitation if they perceive a threat to the colony.

- Honeybees understand that hard times happen and they are always prepared for short-term interruptions of supply as well as the more predictable seasonal shortages.

- Honeybees share: they know there is plenty

of food out there for everyone, including other bees and other pollinating insects. Honeybees do not compete head-on with other species: there is overlap in their food sources, but they do not need to drive others from their territory.

- Honeybees adapt to their surroundings. This extends even to their use of propolis, which varies according to local conditions, and can protect them against localized pathogens.

- Honeybees behave as if they understand that honest communication is at the heart of community. Bees are highly effective communicators, using vibrations and pheromones to pass complex messages around their colony. As far as we know, they are incapable of telling anything but the truth as they understand it.

- Honeybees' survival depends on selecting high quality, untainted food from a variety of sources. Because we have assumed control of much of their territory for our own purposes, we are responsible for ensuring that they continue to have access to flowers untainted by toxic chemicals, against which they have no defence.

For almost all of the last 130 million years or so, bees have had flowering plants pretty much to themselves. In the last 100 years, their entirely organic, natural diet has been contaminated with substances they can never before have encountered: man-made chemicals designed to poison them and their kind, some of them cunningly incorporated into the living chemistry of the plants they feed on. More and more of these toxins are being spread on crops and on the soil and the bees have no chance of surviving their onslaught unless we intervene right now.

If we care about the survival of the honeybee, we must radically reform our farming and food production methods. The alternative is a world dominated by a handful of powerful corporations, intent on bringing the food chain completely under their control, heedless of the fate of thousands of species of birds, bees and other creatures that will be eliminated if we allow them to have their way.

Ten Things You Can Do

Here are some things you can do to help the bees, other pollinators and wildlife in general:

1. Stop using insecticides - especially for 'cosmetic' gardening

There are better ways of dealing with pests - especially biological controls. Modern pesticides are extremely powerful and many are long-lasting and very toxic to bees and other insects. A surfeit of pests can also be seen as a shortage of predators - the basis of many biological controls. *Removing all unnecessary pesticides from the environment is probably the single most important thing we can do to help save the bees.*

2. Create your own Bee-Friendly Zone

By doing two simple things – avoiding insecticides and herbicides, and creating habitat by planting bee-friendly flowers – you can create a Bee-Friendly Zone as small as a window-box or as big as a public park, a whole village or neighbourhood. Every BFZ represents a small victory for bees and removes one more piece of land from the Toxic Zone.

3. Read the labels on garden compost - beware hidden killers!

Some garden and potting composts are on sale that contain Imidacloprid - a deadly, systemic insecticide manufactured by Bayer. It is often disguised as 'vine weevil protection' or similar, but it is highly toxic to all insects and all soil life, including beneficial earthworms. The insecticide is taken up by plants, and if you use this compost in hanging baskets, bees seeking water from the moist compost may be killed.

4. Create natural habitat

If you have space in your garden, let some of it go wild to create a safe haven for bees and other insects and small mammals. Gardens that are too tidy are not so wildlife-friendly. Land awaiting development is also a good place to encourage bee-friendly plants, as is marginal land that has fallen out of use.

5. Plant bee-friendly flowers

You can buy wildflower seeds from many seed merchants, and they can be sown in any spare patch of ground - even on waste ground that is not being cultivated. Some 'guerilla gardeners' even plant them in public parks and waste ground!

6. Provide a site for beehives

If you have some space to spare, you could offer a corner of your garden to a local 'natural beekeeper' as a place to keep a hive or two. They will need to have regular access, so bear this in mind when considering a site.

7. Make a wild bee house

Providing a simple box as a place for feral bees to set up home is one step short of taking up beekeeping, but may appeal to those who want to have bees around but don't want to get involved with looking after them. If you follow sensible guidelines, you can make a box they can live in for a number of years without interference.

8. Support your local beekeepers

Many people believe that local honey can help to reduce the effects of hay fever and similar allergies, which is one good reason to buy honey from a local beekeeper rather than from supermarkets, most of which source honey from thousands of miles away. If you can, find a beekeeper who does not use any chemicals in their hives and ask for pure comb honey from a 'natural beekeeper' for a real treat.

9. Learn about bees - and tell others

Bees are fascinating creatures that relatively few people take the trouble to understand. Read a good book about bees and beekeeping, and who knows - you might decide to -

10. Become a (natural) beekeeper

It is easier than you might imagine to become a beekeeper - and you don't need any of the expensive equipment in the glossy catalogues! Everything you need to keep bees successfully can be made by anyone with a few simple tools: if you can put up a shelf, you can probably build a beehive.

Bee-friendly zones

Since the first stories began to appear in the popular press about so-called 'Colony Collapse Disorder', there has been an enormous amount of public support for the general proposition of 'saving the bees'.

As usual, news media focused on the more sensational aspects of the story and leaped on all manner of outlandish theories about the likely cause, regularly invoking a mythical 'quote' from Einstein, which predicted the imminent demise of the human race within a few years of the disappearance of the bees.

Blame for the problem was laid variously at the doors of aliens, high-altitude 'chemical trails' from commercial aircraft and cell phone masts, while the most obvious culprits - agricultural insecticides, herbicides, genetically modified crops, habitat loss, pollution, and the industrial-scale abuse of bees by commercial bee farmers -

were mostly ignored, except by a handful of campaigners who had foreseen something of this sort as an inevitable consequence of our degraded and deteriorating relationship with the natural world.

As scientists began to find an alarming variety of pesticides inside beehives, which had either been innocently brought in with pollen and nectar by bees foraging on treated farm crops, or deliberately introduced by beekeepers attempting to deal with pests and diseases, it became increasingly clear even to some of the lazier journalists that the story of the disappearing bees was part of a much bigger and scarier picture. Bees began to be seen as the 'canary in the coal mine', warning us what could happen to many other species if we failed radically to change our thoughtless, destructive ways.

Predictably, the agri-pharma-biotech corporations - now invoking Orwell by calling themselves the 'Crop Protection Industry' - denied that any of their products were remotely to blame. Likewise, denials of responsibility came from the perpetrators of genetically modified crops and those responsible for the erection of cell phone masts. The public became confused, the regulators refused to act or to admit that they were powerless and the corporates continued to make a fat profit.

So now we know that governments are unwilling to take a stand against their corporate paymasters, it is up to us to change things; literally from the ground up. We can each of us create a Bee-Friendly Zone on any patch of land that is within our control.

A Bee-Friendly Zone is an act of rebellion against those who would smother our land with toxic chemicals and a positive act of support for our bees. It is a safe place where bees and other insects can nest, forage for pollen and nectar and go about their business.

A BFZ can be a small as a balcony or patio - even a window box - or as big as a public park, a village, a farm, a neighbourhood or even a town or city.

Find out more about Bee-Friendly Zones at
www.beefriendlyzone.org

Find out more about natural beekeeping at
www.biobees.com

Lightning Source UK Ltd.
Milton Keynes UK
UKOW051511290113

205558UK00001B/3/P